Friendship

101 Ways To Be A Better Friend

Paige Jeary

Carpenter's Son Publishing

Friendship: 101 Ways to Be a Better Friend

Copyright © 2011 by Paige Jeary

Published by Carpenter's Son Publishing, Franklin, Tennessee

Published in association with Larry Carpenter of Christian Book Services, LLC
www.christianbookservices.com

Cover Design by: Debbie Manning Shepphard

Interior Layout by: Suzanne Lawing

Edited by: David D. Troutman

Printed in the United States of America

978-0-9832846-7-3

Table of Contents

Chapter 3: Building a Strong Friendship 39

29. Be a *1 Corinthians 13* kind of friend.
30. Be a loyal friend.
31. Prove yourself trustworthy.
32. Be there! A true friend will stand by, even in times of trouble.
33. Convince your friend that she is valuable.
34. Be a "Barnabas" friend (encourager).
35. Tell her—in love—when she is wrong, and ask her to do the same with you.
36. Give a gift—for no reason!
37. Write encouraging notes.
38. Be the first to seek peace when you disagree.
39. Learn how to talk through disagreements.
40. Forgive once, then twice, and then lose count.
41. Get to know your friend's family.
42. Step in when your friend needs help.
43. Pray for your friend.
44. Write a poem describing your friend.
45. Be sensitive.
46. Laugh together—a lot!
47. Take your friend with you on a family trip.
48. Make her birthday special.
49. Go to church camp together.
50. Share your favorite books.
51. When you go on a trip, send her a postcard.
52. Be happy for your friend's successes.
53. Keep in touch when life keeps you apart.
54. Risk sharing your true feelings.
55. Be reliable.
56. Learn something new together.
57. Be flexible and keep a positive spirit.
58. Appreciate your differences and learn the art of compromise.
59. Don't take her for granted.
60. Do a Bible study together.
61. Enjoy being spontaneous together.
62. Learn to enjoy the moment.

Chapter 4: Making Forever Friends 73

63. A cord of three strands is not quickly broken (Ecclesiastes 4:9).
64. Believe in your friend when she doesn't believe in herself.
65. Best friends listen to what you don't say.
66. Make a BFF scrapbook.

67. Celebrate often!
68. Write a song together about your friendship.
69. Talk deeper than feelings: bare your inmost souls.
70. Start some traditions together.
71. Make a BFF "living" collage.
72. Dream and set goals together.
73. Write your BFF story.
74. Make a BFF movie.
75. Put together a time capsule.
76. Hold each other accountable.
77. Pray together often.
78. Help each other grow farther than you've been before.
79. Apply unfailing love.
80. Make a team presentation about BFF to your Sunday school class.
81. Look through each other's old family scrapbooks, photo albums, and yearbooks.
82. Base your friendship on commitment rather than feelings.
83. Go on a "Goodwill" adventure.
84. Prepare and serve a BFF parents' dinner.
85. Make a BFF painting.
86. Make some BFF bracelets and sell them for charity.
87. Plant a BFF tree.
88. Plan a high school graduation trip together.
89. It's okay to have more than one BFF.
90. Forever friends hold a piece of your heart.

Chapter 5: Friendship Nuggets from True BFF Stories   101

91. Mary and Elizabeth: God knows your need of friendship.
92. My Friend Blair: Best friends often feel like family.
93. Logan and Olivia: A true friend encourages you to be everything God wants you to be.
94. David and Jonathan: Best friends make sacrifices for each other.
95. My Friend Katie: Great friends watch out for each other.
96. Hannah and Emily: Best friends are there for you in the worst of times.
97. Ruth and Naomi: Best friends understand that sometimes friends say things they don't mean.
98. My Friend Abbi: Happiness is contagious!
99. My Friend Hannah: Good friends make their friends feel comfortable.
100. My Friend Alli: A good friend will remain loyal and defend your character.
101. Paul and Timothy: Great friends will bring each other joy.

Foreword

The moment this little blonde-headed girl entered my second grade classroom, I knew I was going to be blessed. She was a gift from God. Paige entered my life with a smiling face, shy and reserved, but with the confidence of an older child. She was eager to give me a hug, but she did not say a word. I knew right then that this sweet child was something very special.

As I began to get to know this seven-year-old child and she began to know me, a bond began to form. I watched as she played and learned. I noticed strengths, and I noticed what some would call "struggles." I was blessed to watch a very special little girl grow up.

In the second grade, Paige struggled with reading and writing. She never gave up.

In the second grade, Paige saw the needs of others. She never gave up. I watched that year as her parents tried to understand the struggles Paige was going through with her school work and with finding that "one true girlfriend." I knew that Paige was wonderful and that she had a purpose, and most importantly I knew that God would work everything together for good for those who love Him. I knew that Paige loved God.

Paige often spoke to me about the love she had for her mom and dad, her sister, and her grandparents. More often, though, she would tell me about her love for Jesus. Paige did not use words to touch lives in second grade—she used her life. In everything she did, she showed love. In the determination to complete a school assignment, in showing no favoritism toward a classmate, and in loving all the people in her life, she emulated Jesus Christ. I recognized that a special child had been brought into my life.

When the year ended, I had to say goodbye. She moved on to third grade and to a new teacher. I knew I would miss not being blessed by her smile each morning. But again, I watched God work all things together for good for those who love Him and are called according to His purpose. I simply obeyed the Lord when He placed the opportunity for a grade move into my life, and, when we say "yes" to God, we are blessed. I became Paige's teacher once again—in the fifth grade.

Several years have passed since the day we said goodbye on that last day of second grade, but it seems like yesterday. Paige is the same special girl I met that one morning years ago, just older and taller. She is the same sweet spirit, the same loving friend, and the same girl who puts Jesus first in all she does. The only difference is that Paige no longer has the struggles she endured in the second grade. With perseverance and love from her family, Paige has become a strong, confident, and loving young lady.

I know that God created Paige to do a mighty work here on earth. I believe He is using her to be the bond that will unite person to person. I believe His plan and purpose for Paige is to show the love and light of Christ to those in need.

May you be blessed by this book and the message it contains.

With the love of Christ and many blessings,
Kathi Melo

Introduction

I have been blessed to grow up in a family that really encourages servanthood and making friends. Through that encouragement, I have grown to realize the power of friendship. I have worked with my father and his colleagues to put this book together in hopes that it will be of value to many who read it. I truly hope you enjoy it.

Paige Jeary

Chapter 1: Making Friends

1. True friendship is a gift. Cherish it.

I once read a quote by an unknown author that said, "Friends are God's way of taking care of us." He made us to have close relationships with other people and with Him. True friendships are really special. A true friend is one:

- You enjoy being with.
- You can be yourself with.
- You can tell anything to and know she won't tell anyone else.
- Who will love you no matter what.
- Whom you respect and who respects you back.
- Who will be there when you need her, even during the bad times.
- Who is honest with you and with others.

2. Knowing who you are will help you choose the right friends.

God made us all unique individuals, with our own personalities, gifts, and talents. We have all had different life experiences and relationships. The more we know about ourselves, the easier it will be to find the right friends. The most important thing to know is that God loves you and that you are His child.

What is important to you? God? Family? Honesty? Loyalty? *What interests you?* Sports? Theater? Youth group? Music? Animals? Gymnastics? Movies? *What things have affected your life the most?* Relationships? The Bible? A family move? The addition or loss of a family member? Even though we are all different, many close friendships come from shared interests or experiences.

3. To make a friend, you have to be a friend.

Friendships don't usually just happen. It's easier to start a friendship when you act friendly. You can always start out with a smile. It's easier than it sounds.

You may need to start the conversation by just saying "hi" and asking, "Have you lived here long?" Relax and think about the other person instead of focusing on yourself. Look back at the qualities of a true friend listed on page 4. If you become that kind of a friend yourself, you may find that you have many true friends.

"A man who has friends must himself be friendly."—Proverbs 18:24 (KJV)

4. It takes courage to make a new friend.

It can be scary trying to make new friends. But with God's help, you can overcome your fear. The Bible says God has not given you a spirit of timidity. That's good news! God didn't make you shy. It's something you can overcome! Practice smiling to yourself in the mirror, saying "hi," and starting a conversation. God has given you a spirit of power (the inward kind of strength to do what you need to do), love (that allows you to think more about the other person and less about your fear), and self-discipline (the ability to keep trying until it works).

"For God did not give us a spirit of timidity, but a spirit of power, of love and of self-discipline."— 2 Timothy 1:7

5. Your friends reflect who you are. Choose wisely.

A Japanese proverb says, "When the character of a man is not clear to you, look at his friends." It's great to be friendly to everyone, but when it comes to choosing your close friends, be careful. Would you want someone to mistake your best friend for you? Doesn't it make sense to choose friends whose influence on you will be good? It's hard to break up a friendship, so it's best to choose wisely the first time. Make a list of the qualities you are looking for in a friend. As you get to know people, you will be able to tell if they have those qualities. And talk to your parents. Get them involved and ask for their advice, because they have a lot of wisdom and they've been through the same situations you are going through.

6. Be open to friendships from unexpected people.

If we think all of our friends have to be just like us, we may overlook people who look or seem different. We may be looking on the outside instead of on the inside, where the true person is. For example, you may be surprised to find that people from a different culture are very much like you on the inside. Just think about how lonely and scared you would be if you were in a strange culture with no friends. It would be fun to find out things about their culture: their customs, what they eat, and how they celebrate holidays. You could explain to them why we celebrate Thanksgiving, Christmas, and Easter in America. You may be the very first person to tell them about Jesus!

7. Make different kinds of friends. They are all valuable.

   Open your heart, and God will show you the best in many friends: One friend you can be silly with, another who lifts you up when you're down; another who cheers you on when you're trying something new, and another who is your best shopping buddy. One friend you love to just hang out with and be yourself. One you can talk with about spiritual things. Another who shares your love for movies, and another your love for the sports you enjoy. These may all be wrapped up in one friend, but usually they're wrapped up in several: one from third grade, one from seventh, several from church, a couple from camp. On some days your mom, on others your sister, on others your neighborhood friend. Whether they've been your friends for 10 minutes or 10 years, God has placed them in your life to make a difference.[1]

[1] Based on "Girls in My Circle" email, author unknown, received 5/10/08

8. Get to know someone before you judge her.

Have you ever heard, "Don't judge a book by its cover"? Sometimes we form an opinion about someone from what we see on the outside instead of what is on the inside. Our first impression may not always be correct. We may also be influenced by what someone else says about a person instead of getting to know her for ourselves. Spend time getting to know her, focusing on her good points instead of her weaknesses. Remember to balance this with choosing your friends cautiously. If you still think you can't be good friends, continue to love her and encourage her to grow in her strengths.

"If you judge people, you have no time to love them."—Mother Teresa

9. Be kind. Kindness often draws friends.

Author Leo Buscaglia says, "Too often we underestimate the power of a touch, a smile, a kind word, a listening ear, an honest compliment, or the smallest act of caring, all of which have the potential to turn a life around." Kindness is powerful. This is what a guy named Jeff experienced when his school started a Random Acts of Kindness Week: "I learned that in order for Random Acts of Kindness Week to work for me, I needed to step outside myself and think of others and enjoy the time I spend with them. I really came out of my comfort zone during the week, and I also made a few new friends! …By being kind, I was rewarded with hugs, new friends, and the feeling a person gets when they give for no reason."[2]

[2]High School Kindness, http://www.actsofkindness.org/sites/default/files/pdfs/211_pdf.pdf (accessed 1/27/09)

10. Be yourself.

Don't try to be someone you are not or make up lies to try to impress people. For example, don't say you play basketball when you are really more into volleyball or piano. People can usually see through that, and they will respect you more if you are real. Being fake is being dishonest—both with yourself and others. Being yourself means you have to know who you are and like who you are, and sometimes that means making some changes. God made you special and unique, and He will help you be the very best you that you can be. If you need some help, talk to a friend or an adult you respect, like a youth pastor, a Sunday school teacher, your parents, or a special teacher at school.

11. Your body language speaks for you.

Body language is what we communicate with our facial expressions, our eyes, the way we stand, and our gestures. What we say with our body language sometimes speaks louder—or different—than what we say with our mouths. We may say we are happy, for example; but if we forgot to tell our face that, it may be saying something else. We may be smiling with our lips but not with our eyes. Or we may want our friend to think we are listening, but our eyes are going everywhere around the room but on her face. Be as aware of what you are communicating with your body language as you are with your words. When they match, it helps people to trust you more.

12. Give sincere compliments.

What we say—and how we say it—has a huge impact on our friends and family. Proverbs 18:21 says, "The tongue has the power of life and death." We can make others feel great by giving them sincere compliments, or we can destroy their confidence by saying something negative. It's usually pretty easy to compliment a friend when she has done something really well or is trying hard to do something new. But it's not always so easy when she messes up or you don't think she will succeed. Find something to compliment her about, even if you praise her for her hard work and effort. When you make a habit of giving genuine compliments, you can make people feel good about themselves, and it will make you feel great, too.

13. Get involved in activities you enjoy to meet new friends.

If you want to meet new friends you will have a lot in common with, get involved in the activities you love.

- Join a swim club or the YMCA.
- Get active in youth activities at your church.
- Sign up for dance, gymnastics, or cheerleading.
- Play a sport: tennis, soccer, basketball, volleyball, or baseball.
- Join a club: Good News Club, Chess Club, or another after-school group.
- Start a Bible study.
- Join the school band.
- Work out at the gym.

14. Use your gift for intimacy to include others.

Exclusion is more of a girl thing than it is a guy thing, and the rejection from it can be pretty painful. We have a tendency to draw a tight circle of intimacy around our close friends and exclude others. Most girls our age probably know what it feels like to be excluded from one of these circles at least once, and it's not fun. Sometimes our sense of worth is all tied up with being popular, and we can fall into the trap of excluding others just to be a part of the group. God wants us to use our gift for intimacy to express love and encouragement to others—not to cause them pain. The next time you are tempted to go along with the crowd and exclude someone, turn it into an opportunity to make a new friend.

15. Put your trust in God instead of people.

If you have experienced the pain of exclusion, or if you feel hurt or betrayed by your friends for any other reason, remember that your sense of worth is not tied to your relationships with friends but with God. He loves you and will never leave you. When you learn to put your complete trust in Him instead of in people, you will experience His unconditional love. People will fail you; God never will—no matter what you do. When you understand how much He loves you, you can more easily love others and share His love with them.

16. Listen for God's nudges. He may be showing you a special friend.

Someone described her special friendship like this: "We've shared so much laughter, so many tears. We're a spiritual bond that grows stronger each year. We're not sisters by birth, but we knew from the start, God put us together to be sisters by heart." Sometimes when you meet someone new, you know that it was God who put you together. You almost seem like best friends right away. You seem to flow together in spirit. You understand each other. You just know it's going to be an awesome friendship put together by an awesome God.

Chapter 2: Getting to Know New Friends

17. Value your relationships.

Life is really about relationships—with God, our family, our friends, and others God has placed in our lives. You will probably agree with me that relationships are the most important part of our lives. How awesome is it that our relationship with God is one that we can depend on no matter what! He's blessed us with loving families. And He's the one who brings special people into our lives and helps us develop close relationships with friends. Let's remember to be grateful for them and show we care by giving them our love, our time, and our encouragement to be all they can be.

18. Invite a New Friend to Spend One-on-One Time with You

Friendship is usually built on time shared with each other. It's hard to get to know someone well in the small bites of time you get to spend together at school or church. Talking on the phone and texting are great, but there is something about spending time face-to-face that brings things to a more personal level. Ask your new friend over and go for a long walk. Being outdoors is good for you, and it's a great place to talk and still have enough distractions to fill any awkward gaps in the conversation. If that's not an option, get out a favorite scrapbook or photo album and talk around the memories, being sure to allow your friend plenty of time to share and you plenty of time to listen.

19. Have a Slumber Party

What better way to get to know several new friends than having a slumber party? Ask for phone numbers from two or three girls you would like to get to know better, and then call them at home to invite them. All the moms may even want to meet for coffee so they can get to know each other, too! You may want to start out with something special—like going ice-skating, cooking homemade pizza, or watching a movie. Then put on some great Christian music and have some "girl time" to get to know each other. Give each other a manicure and try different hairstyles. Keep things fun and positive and be careful not to pair up and exclude others. You want to make sure all of your guests have a great time!

20. Play let's-get-acquainted games.

A fun and easy way to get to know new friends is to play one of those cool games you get on email all of the time. You know, the ones that ask what color of socks you have on and what was the last movie you watched! Or you may want to make one up yourself that simply asks preferences, like "Sports or dance? Math or Art? Bananas or Strawberries?" They will give you a glimpse into each other's personalities, and you may be surprised at the way they open up really good conversation. Be sure not to ask awkward or embarrassing questions.

21. Avoid Gossip.

Sometimes when we are getting to know a new friend, it is tempting to gossip about someone else. Maybe we think that making ourselves look good and someone else look bad will make our new friend like us better. But that's one of the most harmful things we can do! Not only does it hurt the person we are talking about, but it also sends a message to our new friend that we can't be trusted. There's nothing wrong with talking about other people—as long as we say something good about them. You know, our moms really do have good advice for us, especially when they say things like, "If you can't say something good about someone, don't say anything at all."

22. Be a great listener.

Really listening is a great way to show your friend you care about her. Someone who listens well:

- Keeps good eye contact

- Doesn't interrupt

- Pays close attention to what her friend is saying

- Waits until her friend finishes to start thinking about her next point

- Asks questions or makes comments after her friend is through talking to show she is interested in what she said.

23. Be a good leader, but know when to follow.

    Usually when a group of two or more friends get together, there is at least one person in the group who has a bigger influence than others on what the group does. A good leader has confidence about where she is going, listens carefully to what the others have to say, and then helps the group make wise choices. Even if you are new to the group, you can use your influence to lead others in the right direction. Sometimes it's best for a good leader to be a follower when someone else has a great idea or even when the group just wants to go a different direction that is not harmful.

24. Don't try too hard. Rushing a friendship can ruin it.

Sometimes it's tempting to "claim" someone as your best friend before the friendship has had a chance to grow to that point. It's important to let things develop naturally instead of trying to rush it. You can let her know you think she's special without making demands that will overwhelm her. Being possessive of your new friend's time or showering her with too much of your attention can sometimes ruin the friendship instead of making it better. Relax and spend some time just getting to know each other. Allow time to build mutual trust and respect and just let the friendship "happen."

25. Allow your friends to have other friends.

The coolest act of friendship is to allow your friends to have other friends. When you insist on having a "best friend" and then get upset if she wants to have other friends, you are setting your friendship up to fail. In Galatians 5:16, jealousy is listed as one of the "acts of the sinful nature"—something you want to be sure and avoid. There is nothing wrong with both of you having other friends. That doesn't mean that you don't care about each other. It just means that you have enough confidence in yourselves to understand that friendship is a gift to be shared.

26. Don't expect perfection.

If you're looking for a perfect friend, you will never find her. Everyone makes mistakes—even you! Looking for a friend who lives up to all of your expectations only leads to disappointment. Allow your friends to fail and then forgive them and encourage them. Remember, it may be you who needs understanding and forgiveness the next time. Look beyond the disappointment and keep your eye on the real goal—making good friends. The Bible tells us that "love covers a multitude of sins" (1 Peter 4:8). When you care more about the person than the offense, you can overlook many of the little things that come up.

27. Show that you really care.

Often it's the little things that build a friendship. Show your new friend you care (without overwhelming her) by doing thoughtful things like:

- Noticing and complimenting her new hairstyle
- Sharing a treat from your lunch
- Calling her when she's sick
- Offering to help with a difficult paper or subject in school
- Praying for her during a test
- Cheering her up when she's down.

28. Work together on a community or church project.

One way to get to know a person really quickly is to work with them on a project. It's usually way more fun to do something with a friend, and there are plenty of worthwhile projects that need to be done. Invite a new friend to volunteer with your youth group at a local food pantry, to do yard work for an elderly person in your neighborhood, or to make cookies for the youth bake sale at church. Meeting the needs of others can bring out the best in people, and it will give you a chance to bond with a friend who hopefully has a servant's heart to match yours!

Chapter 3:
Building a Strong
Friendship

29. Be a *1 Corinthians 13* kind of friend.

Strong friendships are built on love. For the words "love" and "it" in this scripture passage, substitute the words "a friend," and you will see a beautiful description of the best kind of friendship: "Love is patient, love is kind. It does not envy, it does not boast, it is not proud. It is not rude, it is not self-seeking, it is not easily angered, it keeps no record of wrongs. Love does not delight in evil but rejoices with the truth. It always protects, always trusts, always hopes, always perseveres"—1 Corinthians 13:4-7. This kind of friendship is strong because it puts all of the focus on loving the other person rather than on watching out for your own rights.

30. Be a loyal friend.

Strong friendships are based on loyalty. In his book *The Loyalty Effect,* Fred Reichheld defines loyalty as the willingness to make an investment or personal sacrifice to strengthen a relationship.[3] At our age, it's tempting to be "best friends" with a different person every week or so, depending on our moods and how well our friends "perform." Too often we aren't willing to make the personal sacrifice needed to strengthen the relationship with our friends. When others try to pull us away, we don't stand faithfully by our friends or true to our relationships. We need to be willing to be "sticky" friends: friends that stick together and stick up for each other.

[3] Aaron Green, "What is Loyalty and How Do You Develop It?" boston.com, http://www.boston.com/jobs/on_staffing/022007.shtml (accessed 3/11/09).

31. Prove yourself trustworthy.

Strong friendships are based on trust. To prove yourself trustworthy, be very careful to tell the truth and to not break a promise you make to your friends or repeat something they have told you in confidence. If you betray a friend's trust, it is very hard to gain it back again. So even if it seems difficult, it's always best to have the integrity and courage to do the right thing to start with. When you prove yourself trustworthy, your friends can believe what you say and can respect you. Isn't that the kind of friend you really want to be?

32. Be there! A true friend will stand by, even in times of trouble.

"A friend loves at all times" (Proverbs 17:17).

Difficult times come to everyone, and we all need a good, strong friend to help us get through those tough times. Maybe a good friend is going through a difficult problem at home, or she didn't make cheerleader or the soccer team. Or maybe she did something that she knows was really dumb and she is having to pay the consequences. Don't abandon her. This is a time when she needs you the most. Do something kind for her to cheer her up, and let her know you will be there for her and help in any way you can. Your friendship will come out much stronger on the other side.

33. Convince your friend that she is valuable.

A friend may need a boost in her self-esteem from time to time, especially if someone has put her down or she has gone through a humiliating situation. Make it your mission to convince her that she is valuable. She needs to know that she is precious to God—and to you. Show her all the things that make her special. She may have a sense of humor that won't quit or a compassion for others. Or she may have a servant's heart or a love for children. Help her to see her strengths and her worth, first to the One that counts most, and then to her friends and family and others in her world. Really, it's good to show our friends how valuable they are to us all of the time, even when things are going well.

34. Be a "Barnabas" friend (encourager).

A man named Joseph was a follower of Jesus, but the apostles called him Barnabas, which means *Son of Encouragement* (Acts 4:36). Barnabas was the one who convinced the apostles not to be afraid of Saul (Paul) after God changed him on the road to Damascus. And Barnabas was the one the apostles sent to Antioch to encourage the new believers there to remain true to the Lord with all their hearts (Acts 11:23). You can be a Barnabas to your friends, encouraging them to be strong in their faith and remain true to the Lord, no matter what they are going through.

35. Tell her—in love—when she is wrong, and ask her to do the same with you.

"Wounds from a friend can be trusted…" (Proverbs 27:6).

If strong friendships are based on love, loyalty, and trust, then honesty has to play a big part, as well. A true friend will tell her friend when she is wrong. Here's the catch: your only motivation can be love. It may not always be easy, but it's the right thing to do. If a friend is being rude to someone else or even putting herself down, you can pick the right time when you are alone to lovingly point that out to her. She may not realize she is doing it. Or if you have a bad attitude about a situation, be grateful when your friend points that out to you. Understand that she is telling you only because she cares about you.

36. Give a gift—for no reason!

A great way to show a friend that you value her friendship is to give her a gift for no reason. It shows her that you were thinking about her and wanted to surprise her with something that would make her happy. Don't overdo it, of course, but a small, inexpensive gift once in a while just to show her she is special can mean a lot. It can be a treat you know she loves, like a piece of your mom's chocolate cake, or it can be something you know she collects or a book she would enjoy. Everyone likes to feel special and loved.

37. Write encouraging notes.

It's a girl thing, no matter what age. Almost all girls enjoy sending encouraging notes or cards, and we love to get them. Dee Brestin, author of *The Friendships of Women*, said her daughter Sally received a note like this from her friend Shelli. Isn't it a cool note to give to a friend?

[4] Dee Brestin, *The Friendships of Women* (Colorado Springs: Cook Communications Ministries, 2001), 16.

38. Be the first to seek peace when you disagree.

Most good friends will have disagreements from time to time. It's great if you can ask God to help you be the peacemaker and make the first move. Confiding in others first before talking to your friend only puts them in the middle and makes the problem worse, and it is not fair to your friend. It would be hard for other friends to give advice anyway, without hearing both sides of the story, and you want to avoid causing them to take up an offense for you or against your friend. It's best to pray and ask God to give you the courage to go to your friend and see if you can talk through the disagreement.

39. Learn how to talk through disagreements.

There is a way to talk through disagreements without breaking up the friendship, especially if you are both followers of Christ. The first thing you need to do is agree to talk—and really listen—to each other. Remember to speak in love and with respect, without letting your emotions take over. State your feelings clearly and avoid saying things like "you never" or "you always." Make sure your friend has a chance to talk without your interrupting her, and take turns until you both have a clear understanding of the problem. Sometimes it's simply a case of misunderstanding, or other times you may need to agree to disagree. Whatever the case, be ready to be the first to forgive.

40. Forgive once, then twice, and then lose count.

"Then Peter came to Jesus and asked, "Lord, how many times shall I forgive my brother when he sins against me? Up to seven times?" Jesus answered, "I tell you, not seven times, but seventy-seven times"—Matthew 18:21-22. The point Jesus was making in these verses is not that we are to keep track of how many times we forgive—and then stop at seventy-seven—but that we are to lose count along the way and never stop forgiving. Sometimes it's hard to forgive, but it's always best. Friends who learn to forgive a lot have a strong friendship!

41. Get to know your friend's family.

   Showing a friend that you are interested in her family and want to get to know them is a great way to build a strong friendship. Our families are important to us, and in many ways they have shaped who we are today. So when you express an interest in getting to know your friend's family, you are saying, "I want to know you better and be a part of what is important to you." When we have a great relationship with each other's families, it strengthens the bond between us. Our parents usually love it because it creates a sense of trust and allows them to be more involved in our lives.

42. Step in when your friend needs help.

Friendship is about loving and caring and sharing. If your friend has a big project to do, show her you care by offering to share her load. She may have a project at school that she needs help with, or her mom may have asked her to clean out her closet. She may have volunteered for a project for a club or her youth group. Jump in and do what you can to help. A big job is much easier with a friend's help—and it's a lot more fun! If there is something in it for you (like getting more time with your friend later to do something fun), that's great. But if you do it when there is nothing in it for you, your friend will really understand the depth of your friendship.

43. Pray for your friend.

Praying for your friends is the very best thing you can do for them. When you pray for someone, you are making an investment in her life. Not only does it show you care, but it also shows you trust God to watch over her, help her, and bless her. We face many temptations at our age, so it would be great to ask God to help your friend resist temptation and stay pure in her thoughts, words, and actions. Let your friend know you are praying for her, and ask her to pray for you, too!

44. Write a poem describing your friend.

One way to let a friend know she is special is to write a poem about her. List the things you love about her, and then write it into a poem (it doesn't have to rhyme). Tell her why you admire her. You might start with the fruit of the spirit (Galatians 5:22-23). Do the qualities of love, joy, peace, patience, kindness, goodness, faithfulness, gentleness and self-control show in her life? Does she have the gift of making others feel good about themselves? Is she generous? Loving? Compassionate? Strong? Just start thinking about her qualities and writing them down. If it doesn't end up as a poem, that's okay. She would enjoy prose as well.

45. Be sensitive.

Sometimes when we're cutting up with our friends, it's easy
to hurt someone's feelings without really meaning to. We may,
without thinking, poke fun at someone for something she did or
said or worse, for the way she looks. Friendships can rise and fall at
moments like this. It's very important to be sensitive to the feelings
of your friends and not humiliate them in front of others. It's equally
important to stand up for someone who has been the brunt of a
comment or joke, or to apologize if you were the one that offended.
You usually know the things your friends are sensitive about, so be
careful not to bring those up in public.

46. Laugh together—a lot!

"A cheerful heart is a good medicine"—Proverbs 17:22.

Laughter is one of the best things you can do for your body. A good laugh:

- Reduces stres
- Distracts from negative emotions
- Leaves a great clean feeling
- Changes our perspective
- Exercises and relaxes muscles
- Connects us with others in a positive way[5]

Laughter is a "positive connection" that helps to make great friendships! Friends who enjoy a lot of good laughs together create happy times and wonderful memories.

[5] Elizabeth Scott, M.S., "The Stress Management and Health Benefits of Laughter: The Laughing Cure," about.com, http://stress.about.com/od/stresshealth/a/laughter.htm (accessed 3/13/09).

47. Take your friend with you on a family trip.

One way to make a good friendship even stronger is to go on a trip together. With your parent's full agreement and permission, of course, invite a good friend to go with you on a family trip. You'll be able to make special memories together, and your friendship will flourish. With that much "together time," there will be opportunities for disagreements, as well, so decide ahead of time that you will respect and enjoy each other while you have this great opportunity. Hopefully your friend has had a chance to get to know your family well, so she will fit right in with all of the silliness and fun of a family trip. Take a lot of pictures!

48. Make her birthday special.

Birthdays are a great opportunity to make a friend feel special. Sometimes it's fun to s-t-r-e-t-c-h out the celebration, especially if you won't get to be with her on "the" day. You might want to give her a card, a note, an e-mail, an e-card, or a text every day for a week before that all lead up to the "big" day. Then make as big a deal of it as she would be comfortable with. You may want to get a group of friends to "serenade" her in the cafeteria, or bring her a fun cookie cake to share, or kidnap her after school and take her to her favorite ice cream place—or all of the above. Whatever it is, make it fun, wacky, memorable, and special. She will feel loved.

49. Go to church camp together.

Some of your best memories come from church camp, so why not make them even more special by sharing the experience with a good friend. Part of the fun will be the anticipation, especially if it's the first time for either or both of you. Be sure to jump in with the rest of the campers and not just be a twosome at camp. Make the most of your experience as you make new friends, enjoy the activities and the outdoors, and allow God to do a deep work in you. Nothing strengthens a friendship more than sharing intimate times with God.

50. Share your favorite books.

If you enjoy reading, good books can be like old friends; and, like old friends, they may be hard to part with. If you have some books that you have really enjoyed or that have helped you grow, share them with your friend. They are just books gathering dust if they are left on the shelves. But if they are shared with a friend, they come to life and become a source of joy and strength. If she knows the book was special to you, it's almost like sharing a part of you with her. It helps her better understand you and strengthens your friendship. And, in the process, you have blessed your friend with the joy of making a "new old friend."

51. When you go on a trip, send her a postcard.

It's fun to get postcards in the mail. Your friend will feel very special if you drop her a card while you are gone, especially when she realizes that you were thinking about her while you were away. Just getting a pretty card with a quick note that says, "Miss you a lot. Wish you were here," will probably make her day. Be sure to take her address and a stamp with you, and mail the card in time to arrive before you return. You may be surprised to someday see your postcard in a scrapbook with other mementos of your friendship!

52. Be happy for your friend's successes.

The true test of friendship may be whether you can celebrate your friend's successes. If you can be happy for her when she gets the part you wanted in the theater production or wins that tenth medal in track, then yours is a strong friendship. Even when you feel that you may live in her shadow or you feel the disappointment of losing to her, enjoy her success with her. All of our talents and strengths come from God, and His plan for you may take you on a completely different path. Resist the temptation to allow jealousy to rear its head, and focus on your awesome friend and why she is so special to you. Just doing that makes you an awesome friend yourself.

53. Keep in touch when life keeps you apart.

Keep your great friendship strong, even when "life" seems to work against you. If one of you moves away or if you are separated for an extended period of time, that doesn't mean you have to let your friendship fall away. Keep in touch. Talk on the phone or by texting or email, but keep the communication flowing. Make plans to visit if at all possible. Send cards and letters of encouragement. Pray for each other. Set "girlfriend dates" to watch a movie at the same time, and call each other after it's over to talk about it. Download free software that allows you to talk on the Internet face to face with web cams. You may just find that your great friendship gets even stronger with the effort you make.

54. Risk sharing your true feelings.

We girls are usually fairly transparent, but we can still sometimes be pretty good at hiding our feelings. When we keep those feelings inside, they usually build into something that's not so pretty—like anger, bitterness, jealousy, or depression. We may think our friends will reject us if we tell them how we really feel. But if we take the risk and trust our good friends with our true feelings, we often find that they are good listeners and want to help us work through things. They may even say they would have been available to help long before, if we had just opened up to them. Risk being vulnerable with your good friends. You will probably find it makes your friendships stronger.

55. Be reliable.

We've said that strong friendships are built on trust. Trust is built on reliability. That means if you tell your friend you will be there to help with a project or will call her on a certain day, or that you will bring her a book you promised, you need to follow through and do what you said. Or if you say you will be somewhere at a certain time, you need to be prompt. If a friend cannot trust your word, she cannot trust that you will be honest with her or that you will not betray her confidence. If you forget from time to time, that is one thing. But constantly failing to follow through on your word is another. If you want strong friendships, be true to your word—consistently.

56. Learn something new together.

The more time you spend with a friend, the more your relationship is strengthened. So why not learn something new together? Even if you do it just for fun, you may actually find a new passion in the process! Here are some things that may be fun to learn together:

- A foreign language (Not one you take in school)
- Art
- Taekwondo
- Play an instrument
- Gymnastics
- Chess
- Horseback riding
- Scrapbooking
- Cooking
- Photography
- Cake decorating
- Acting

57. Be flexible and keep a positive spirit.

Life doesn't always go as we plan. Sometimes we face big disappointments when things don't happen like we want them to. Maybe at the last minute a friend had to cancel plans for shopping and a movie. How did you react? Did you keep a positive outlook and say, "That's okay, we'll go another day"? Getting upset would have only made your friend feel bad, even though she may have had no control over the situation. Being flexible and positive in the face of disappointment helps to strengthen your relationships. It shows your friends that you value them and their feelings more than you do any plans you had made, and they will appreciate your positive attitude.

58. Appreciate your differences and learn the art of compromise.

Even though you may have a lot in common with your good friends, you will probably find some differences, as well. Your best friend may prefer gymnastics and you like piano. Or she may like the beach and you prefer the pool. Appreciate your differences. If you both keep an open mind, you just might learn something from each other. In the meantime, learn the art of compromise. You may want a good salad and she may want a burger. Why not go to the food court at the mall so you can both get what you want? Or make a deal: get a burger this time and make a good salad for lunch tomorrow.

59. Don't take her for granted.

Sometimes we hurt those we are closest to by taking them for granted. Assuming that they will always be there for us, we may not put the effort into making the friendship special. Like any good relationship, friendships require more than 50/50% effort—they require 100/100% effort. In other words, be sure to nurture your friendships and not take advantage of your friends. Most of us have very busy schedules, but at our age we should still have plenty of time for friends. Go the extra mile to see that your friends know they are loved and appreciated, and you will be rewarded with strong friendships.

60. Do a Bible study together.

A really cool way to make a friendship stronger is to do a Bible study together. Find a study that is geared toward teenage girls, or just pick a study on a favorite book of the Bible. Meet together once a week if you can and do as much of the study as you can get through in the time you have allowed. You don't have to be in a hurry. Getting through the book is not necessarily your goal. You want to allow time for meaningful discussions on how this particular portion of the Bible applies to your lives. Or you might prefer to each read a certain passage of scripture during the week and get together to discuss its application.

61. Enjoy being spontaneous together.

Some of the most fun times with friends can be when you do things spontaneously. And at our age, we can usually get by with doing that a lot. There is something about doing things on the spur of the moment that adds to the fun and excitement. Maybe it's the silliness of the moment, but it feels great. It might be just saying the first thing that enters your mind or going outside and singing in the rain together, or doing matching hairstyles. Just be sure the spontaneity is innocent fun and doesn't hurt anyone. Friendship scrapbooks are usually filled with mementos of spontaneous acts!

62. Learn to enjoy the moment.

We are usually so busy during this time of our lives that it would be easy to miss the special moments God gives us with good friends. We need to slow down and really enjoy this awesome time of our lives. When we become adults and have the responsibility of home, family, and work, we won't have the luxury of spending hours hanging out with our best friends, anticipating our future with the excitement of youth. Next time you are with friends you love, stop and look around you, listen to the laughter and conversation, and sense the happiness and contentment you feel. Thank God for the good friends He has given you and the opportunity to strengthen those friendships into lifelong relationships. Enjoy the moment.

Chapter 4:
Making Forever Friends

63. A cord of three strands is not quickly broken.

"Though one may be overpowered, two can defend themselves. A cord of three strands is not quickly broken"— Ecclesiastes 4:12. There is strength in unity. A friendship between two people can be strong, but it is even stronger if there is a third person involved in the friendship—God. If you are bound together in Christ, you are stronger than the two of you by yourselves. A "three-cord" friendship is very likely to be a forever friendship. It may be fun to make each other a three-cord bracelet in honor of your three-cord friendship!

64. Believe in your friend when she doesn't believe in herself.

"A friend is someone who knows the song in your heart and can sing it back to you when you have forgotten the words"—Author Unknown. Life sometimes gets us down—even to the point where we no longer have confidence in ourselves. When your good friend is down or can't seem to take that next step toward a big goal, you may be the one person who can help her. Sometimes you may need to encourage her, reminding her of "the song in her heart." Other times you may need to just be there, listening, and praying. Good friends become forever friends when they never stop believing in each other.

65. Best friends listen to what you don't say.

Another unknown author has said, "Everyone hears what you say. Friends listen to what you say. Best friends listen to what you don't say." A BFF (Best Friends Forever) usually knows you inside and out, sometimes better than you know yourself. When we're upset about something, we may not want to talk about it. But a BFF can usually tell there is something wrong, even when we try to act like there's not. A BFF listens more closely than casual friends. It's not so much what you say that she hears, but what you don't say. If you want your good friend to be your BFF, start listening to what she doesn't say— and then ask her in private if she wants to talk about it.

66. Make a BFF scrapbook.

Remembering happy times together can strengthen friendships, but making a BFF scrapbook gives you the opportunity to relive those fun memories together many times over the years. If you're not yet into Scrapbooking, take a class together or learn from the Internet. Make your book special to the two of you by using your favorite colors and themes. Include pictures, ticket stubs, playbills, programs, cards, letters, notes, pressed flowers, locks of hair, and anything else that captures a happy memory forever. After you complete one, start another one, and keep it going over the years. Look at them together often to keep the memories—and the friendship—fresh.

67. Celebrate often!

So many big things in life deserve a celebration, but when we celebrate even the little things, it just makes life a lot more fun! Celebrate often! Bring out the noisemakers when your best friend gets an A on that test she was dreading, have a "gold medal ceremony" when you master that difficult gymnastics technique, "ring the gong" (hit a pan with a spoon) when she saves enough for an MP3 player, announce her placement on the soccer team with a megaphone—all around the block. Celebrations make the moment more special, keep the memory fresh longer, and even create memories all their own—BFF memories!

68. Write a song together about your friendship.

You know how much fun it is to sing silly songs with your best friend. Why not write a song about your friendship and sing it together! It can be silly or it can be serious—whatever describes your friendship the best. Make it your special song that describes your relationship and some of the fun things you have done or things you have been through together. Sing it often so you will never forget it, and sing it to each other when one of you is down. It's *your* song—one that will always bring to mind your BFF, no matter where life takes you.

69. Talk deeper than feelings: bare your inmost souls.

"I've dreamed of meeting her all my life...a bosom friend—an intimate friend, you know—a really kindred spirit to whom I can confide my inmost soul."—Anne of Green Gables[6]

With good friends, you can talk about your true feelings. But when you find that rare friend you can trust with your inmost soul, that's a BFF. These are friends you can really bare your soul to and trust with your dreams, your hopes—all of those things deep inside of you that make you who you are! Be very careful, though, not to depend on a relationship with a BFF instead of God. He is the only one who will never let you down and who can bring you true peace and joy. When He gives you a soul mate here on this earth, that's a very special gift.

---

[6] L. M. Montgomery, Anne of Green Gables (Boston: L. C. Page and Publishers, 1940), 75.

70. Start some traditions together.

Shared traditions help turn good friendships into BFF friendships. In her book, *Friends: Making Them and Keeping Them*, Patti Criswell suggests that as you spend time together and create lasting memories with traditions, they will become an important part of your friendship. Pick something you both enjoy doing and repeat it over and over again until it becomes a tradition. That may be something as simple as celebrating your birthdays a special way or wearing a certain color on a certain day. Or it may be something silly like having your pictures taken together with the Easter Bunny at the mall every Easter or in a field of wildflowers every spring. Whatever you choose, put forth the effort to continue it over the years to make it a special BFF tradition. [7]

[7] Patti Kelley Criswell, *Friends: Making Them and Keeping Them* (Middleton, WI: American Girl Publishing), 62-65.

71. Make a BFF "living" collage.

If you're a camera bug, you and your BFF may enjoy making a living collage together—one you can keep changing as your memories and friendship grow. Kodak supplied these instructions on the Diynetwork.com web site:

- Plan how you'd like to position the photos.

- Be creative! Crop or overlay some shots if you like, and you can even add captions.

- Then apply the spray mount and start building the collage. Add a few decorative touches and your photos have become a living work of art -- one you can change any time you desire just by switching out the pictures![8]

---

[8] Living Photo Collage, Diynetwork.com, http://www.diynetwork.com/diy/diy_kits/article/0,2019,D IY_13787_2291339,00.html (accessed 3/17/09).

72. Dream and set goals together.

As you dream about the future with your BFF, dare to dream for her—dreams that will help her grow toward her potential in Christ. If she is a good writer, for example, encourage her to send an article to a Christian magazine for publishing. If she has a great voice, convince her to make a demo CD and send it to a Christian recording studio. Dream big and set goals to make those dreams come true. Remember that nothing is impossible with God (Luke 1:37). If He has gifted either of you with a talent, encourage each other to use it to glorify Him.

73. Write your BFF story.

   Your BFF story is special—at least to the two of you. How did
you meet? Did you become friends right away, or did it take a while?
What did you first notice in each other that made you know you
would like to be friends? Were you thrown together at an event?
How long did it take to become BFFs? What did you come to
love about each other? What were some of the special things you
did together? It would be neat to write your story from your two
separate points of view. Who knows? Maybe your story will be an
inspiration for others. At the very least, it will be something you two
can enjoy and can look back on years later and show to your own
children. Wouldn't it be cool if they became BFFs too?

74. Make a BFF movie.

After you write your BFF story, why not act it out—and have someone film it for you? It would be really neat to have a DVD to enjoy for years to come. Get creative. You could take turns narrating and then act out how you met, what made you became really close, and some of the fun things you have done together. Use as many props as you can think of, and even change clothes to create the different scenes. Rehearse until you get pretty good at it, then ask someone—maybe one of your parents—to video it as you act it out. Don't expect it to be perfect, but it could be a lot of fun. And in the process of making the movie, you will create another BFF memory!

75. Put together a time capsule.

Another great suggestion Patti Criswell had in her book, *Friends: Making Them and Keeping Them*, was to make a time capsule together.[9] Get a tube of any kind (a cardboard mailing tube would be the most durable) and place things inside that describe life as it is today and as you think it will be when you open the time capsule. This could include a list of your goals and dreams, your predictions about the future, predictions from your family and friends, and pictures or anything else that shows what is going on in your life today. Seal it with nylon tape and store it in a safe place, and then set a date five or ten years from now to open it with your BFF. (Be sure to keep up with it if you move!).

[9] Patti Kelley Criswell, Friends: Making Them and Keeping Them (Middleton, WI: American Girl Publishing), 66

76. Hold each other accountable.

As best friends, you naturally want to look out for each other. One of the best ways to do that is to be accountable to each other. If she is trying to get better grades, she may want you to check with her often to see if she has improved her study habits. You may ask her to help you eat more healthy foods or have your devotion time with God each day. Being accountable to each other gives you a greater motivation to do the things you want to do to improve your life or keep it on the right track. It's great to have a BFF who is willing to help!

77. Pray together often.

Praying with your BFF is one of the best things you can do together. Friends who pray together generally stay more connected—both emotionally and spiritually. When you pray together, you build a strong spiritual foundation for your friendship. It gives you the opportunity to discuss and pray about the issues you are both facing, the honor of lifting each other up to your Heavenly Father, and the joy of seeing Him work through answered prayers. If you're not comfortable at first, that's okay. Just hold hands and talk to God, one at a time, about the issues your friend is facing. The bonding that often takes place is strong like that "three-cord friendship" we talked about earlier.

78. Help each other grow farther than you've been before.

We are usually attracted to our best friends because we see something in them that we like. Often we see traits that we wish we had ourselves. Maybe you like the way she sees the little things that make life special. And she may see things in you that she wants to be. She may want to develop your gift of understanding people. It's great to have a BFF who inspires us to think and grow beyond where we are now and farther than we have ever grown before.

79. Apply unfailing love.

"What a man desires is unfailing love."—Proverbs 19:22

We all want unfailing love from God and from each other. As Dee Brestin says in *The Friendships of Women*, we really want our best friends to be like family—to love us even if we let them down or move away. It's probably best not to promise unfailing love, because we may not be able to keep that vow. But there can be an unspoken bond between us that says we will nurture the friendship and keep it strong. Christ gives us unfailing love, and if we give unfailing love to our best friends, they just may be our best friends forever. [10]

---

[10] Dee Brestin, The Friendships of Women (Colorado Springs: Cook Communications Ministries, 2001), 126.

80. Make a team presentation about BFF to your Sunday school class.

Has God shown you things in your BFF experience that you could share with others? Have you used some of the ideas in this book to help each other grow spiritually or build a spiritual foundation for your friendship? Ask your Sunday school teacher if you can share those ideas with others in your class to help them grow, as well. If you're a little nervous or lack confidence, my dad has a book called *Purpose-Filled Presentations* that can help you reduce your nervousness and make a great presentation. It will be a great experience for you and your BFF—and for your class!

81. Look through each other's old family scrapbooks, photo albums, and yearbooks.

It's fun to know about your best friend's family and hear some of her family stories. And it's a great way to get more connected to her and her family. Ask her mom to pull out any old family scrapbooks, photo albums, yearbooks, and any other mementos. As you go through them together, try to piece together the family tree. Ask questions to see if some of the great traits you see in your BFF may have been passed down through her family. Then give her the same opportunity with your family mementos. Then you'll both be able to laugh with your families when those inside family jokes come up!

82. Base your friendship on commitment rather than feelings.

Guess what! Your best friend is not perfect, and neither are you! You are both going to reveal weaknesses and make mistakes throughout your friendship, and things may come up from time to time that you don't like about your BFF. *But cherished friendships are built on commitment—not feelings.* There will be a lot of fun times together, but you will hit some rough spots in your friendship at other times. Decide now to base your friendship on commitment rather than feelings so you can make it through those rough spots. The next thing you know, you will be sailing through fun times again!

83. Go on a "Goodwill adventure."

Going on a "Goodwill adventure" with your BFF will be fun, and you will be helping out a great charity at the same time. Go through your closets and drawers together and take out all of the clothes, shoes, handbags, belts, hats, and anything else you find that you no longer wear. (Just think of all the room you will have for new things!) Box everything up neatly and take it to a Goodwill store near you. Take five dollars with you, and you'll be surprised to see what fun you can have finding neat things in the store to bring home— from games to accessories. You will have fun together and help Goodwill—both with your donations and your spending!

84. Prepare and serve a BFF parents' dinner.

Invite both of your parents to a dinner that you and your BFF will prepare and serve. It can be at either home, and it can be as simple as homemade pizza or as nice as lasagna, depending on your cooking abilities. Either way, make it special and fun. Even if you're serving hotdogs, bring out the china, linens, and candles. The idea is to honor your parents and let them know how much you love and appreciate all of them. You two can eat in the kitchen while your parents are having a good time together, but go back in every few minutes and see if they need drink refills. Don't forget the dessert and the music!

85. Make a BFF painting.

I saw a fun idea on the Quazen.com website that I thought would be great thing to do with your BFF. You will need a couple of cheap canvases and some acrylic paint. At the kitchen table, each of you paint on your canvas for about five minutes, and then switch canvases. Do this every five minutes until you finish. It can be a landscape, a "portrait" of the two of you, or any kind of scenery—whatever you like. When you are finished, each piece will have individual art on it from both of you. This can be a lot of fun, even if you don't consider yourself an artist, and both of you will end up with a pretty cool keepsake. [11]

[11] "Creative Things for Teenagers to Do When Bored," Quazen.com, ttp://www.quazen.com/Kids-and-Teens/Entertainment/Creative-Things-for-Teenagers-to-Do-When-Bored.144523 (accessed 3/19/09).

86. Make some BFF bracelets and sell them for charity.

Friendship bracelets are fun to make and fun to wear. Why not get together with your BFF and make a few dozen of them to sell for a charity? You may want to pick a charity that is special to one or both of you. Or it can be a charity that helps children. Maybe there is a family in your church that has a special need. If your cause is big enough, you may want to enlist your families and other friends to help. After the bracelets are made, get the word out about your cause. Your school and church may let you put up flyers or posters, and you can distribute flyers in your neighborhoods. People usually like to rally behind a cause, and you may be surprised at the success of your efforts!

87. Plant a BFF tree.

Want a cool way to help the environment and honor of your BFF friendship? Plant a tree! Planting a tree will:

- Supplement the natural resources of the earth
- Help purify the air
- Bring life and beauty to the area, and
- Memorialize and share the beauty of your friendship with the whole world!

88. Plan a high school graduation trip together.

Whether you will graduate from high school in five years or next year, planning a graduation trip with your BFF can give you something fun and exciting to look forward to together. Ask your parents to set the guidelines, and then create your dream trip to fit within those boundaries. Whether it's a trip to the beach, to the city, or to Europe, half of the fun is dreaming and planning it together. Get travel books, research the Internet for things to do, and get price estimates for travel and hotels. Put everything in a notebook that you can update as you go along. Remember that a lot can change within a few years' time, so be sure to stay flexible and keep your friendship strong.

89. It's okay to have more than one BFF.

Sometimes we are blessed with more than one "soul mate." There may be two or three kindred spirits in your life that you consider your best friends. If you have a special bond with more than one friend that sets them apart from other friends in your life, that's great! It really is healthy to not hold on so tightly to one best friend that we choke the life out of the relationship. By encouraging each other to depend on God first and allowing each other to be open to other friendships He may bring to your life, you may end up with a "circle of best friends"!

90. A forever friend holds a piece of your heart.

A forever friend holds a piece of your heart.
Somehow she's managed to reach right in
And gently respond to that tender spot
That yearns to be cherished and shared.

A forever friend matches up with your soul.
She's your kindred spirit; your hearts commune.
She seals up the cracks and patches the holes
Where life has assaulted and shattered.

A forever friend holds a piece of your heart.
She loves without judging; she earns your trust.
She listens, encourages, forgives, and reveals
Your value to her and to God.

Chapter 5:
Friendship Nuggets
from True BFF Stories

91. Mary and Elizabeth: God knows your need of friendship.

When the angel visited Mary with the message that she would give birth to the Son of God, she received the highest honor possible from God. At the same time, she understood that she would probably be rejected by her fiancé, and possibly by her family. Her cousin Elizabeth was "well along in years" (Luke 1:7) and—until now—had not been able to have children. The angel told Mary about Elizabeth's pregnancy, and Mary recognized God's provision of a friend for her in her time of need. God knew what a tremendous comfort they would be for each other. God knows your need of true friendship, too. Trust Him. [12]

---

[12] Dee Brestin, *The Friendships of Women* (Colorado Springs: Cook Communications Ministries, 2001), 155-158.

92. My friend Blaire: Best friends often feel like family.

When Blaire and I met in third grade, we immediately had a lot in common. We were both coming out of our "tomboy" stage, realizing for the first time how great it was to be a girl! Blaire and I still have so much in common that it sometimes feels like we are sisters. We both love to go eat at nice restaurants, get dressed up and go to fancy places, and shop for cool jewelry and clothes. We can talk about anything—including spiritual things. We even both love volleyball and basketball! I love her family. They make me feel at home—like I am really a part of their family.

93. Logan and Olivia: A true friend encourages you to be everything God wants you to be.

Logan writes: Olivia is my very best friend, and I guess it helps that she is my cousin as well. She moved to Japan for five years, but when she came back, it was like we had never been apart. We recently moved to the town where she lives, and now we do everything together. Olivia is a lot of fun and knows how to be goofy, but when it comes time to be serious, she can help me be serious as well. She is an inspiration to me and makes me want to be a better Christian and a better person. She likes me for me and doesn't try to change who I am, but she encourages me to be everything God wants me to be. I wish everyone could have a friend like Olivia.

94. David and Jonathan: Best friends make sacrifices for each other.

"And Jonathan made a covenant with David because he loved him as himself. Jonathan took off the robe he was wearing and gave it to David, along with his tunic, and even his sword, his bow and his belt"—1 Samuel 18:3-4. Jonathan was the son of a king, next in line for the throne. But he knew that God had anointed David as the next king. Jonathan could have been jealous and wanted to kill David, as his father Saul did. Instead, he realized the wisdom in God's choice and threw all of his love and support behind David—even his own right to the throne. Jonathan wasn't envious of David. He loved him enough to make a huge sacrifice for him. That's how best friends should be.

95. My friend Katie: Great friends watch out for each other.

My friend Katie and I love to be spontaneous together. We make up games, hang out around her neighborhood, or go riding on the golf cart in mine. We enjoy playing sports together, as well. I can go to her with any problem. We are very close, and so are our families. Katie went with me to New York City and our families go to Mexico together every year. (Ask your family about traveling with your friends and their families. It is so much fun!) Katie is a natural leader who draws people to herself. No matter where we go together or what we do, she watches out for everyone. She makes sure everyone is okay and that no one puts anyone down. She's a great friend!

96. Hannah and Emily: Best friends are there for you in the worst of times.

Hannah writes: Emily and I have been through so much together. When I moved to her city with my mom, I didn't know anyone. After a couple of days, she came up to me and asked if I wanted to be friends. We have been inseparable ever since. Almost every summer, she goes to church camp with me. When I moved to another city, she and I still remained best friends, even though there was such a distance between us. When my mother died, she came to be with me. She cried with me and we got through it together. Emily is the best person in the whole world, and I couldn't ask for a better friend.

97. Ruth and Naomi: Best friends understand that sometimes friends say things they don't mean.

Naomi and her family moved to Moab because of a famine in Israel. Naomi's husband died, and her two sons married Moabite women. When both sons died, Naomi decided to go back to Israel; she told both of her daughters-in-law to go home to their mothers. Ruth refused to go. She said to Naomi, "Don't urge me to leave you or to turn back from you. Where you go I will go, and where you stay I will stay. Your people will be my people and your God my God. Where you die I will die, and there I will be buried." (Ruth 1:16-17). Naomi saw how much Ruth loved her, and she stopped asking her to leave. When they got back to Israel, Naomi helped Ruth find a wonderful husband. Sometimes when our friends are hurting, they say things they don't mean. Good friends understand that.

98. My friend Abbi: Happiness is contagious!

Abbi and I have been close friends for a couple of years now, and I have never seen her without a smile. She is one of the happiest people I know, and her happiness is contagious! She makes me and everyone around her happy! Abbi enjoys randomly picking someone to share her happiness with. She will go up to that person and say, "Hi. How is your day going?" She encourages me to get back up when I am down. We can talk about anything! She is very compassionate, but she likes to have fun too. I love to go to her house and goof off or play basketball. Abbi is my "happy friend."

99. My friend Hannah: Good friends make their friends feel comfortable.

Hannah is one of my "early-bird" buddies. We usually get to school early, so we have a chance to hang out and talk about everything. She was shy at first, but after I invited her into the group she became more comfortable around us. Now she is the one who always makes sure everyone is comfortable and okay. Once I tripped over a cord at school while we were rehearsing for a school play and I fell flat out on my face. Everyone started laughing, and I felt so embarrassed. Hannah was one of my friends who took me aside and made me feel better. She's a cool friend to have!

100. My friend Alli: A good friend will remain loyal and defend your character.

Alli is another of my early morning friends. Until fourth grade, I didn't really know her well. But she and I are both tall, and we kept being placed next to each other in line for pictures. So we started talking and became good friends. Alli is one of my quieter friends, but she has proven to be very loyal and trustworthy. One of the girls in my class falsely accused me of calling her names. Alli was one of my friends who stood behind me and said I would never do that. She really helped me get through that bad situation. You always need friends like Alli that you know will stick up for you by telling the truth.

101. Paul and Timothy: Great friends will bring each other joy.

"I thank God…as night and day I constantly remember you in my prayers. Recalling your tears, I long to see you, so that I may be filled with joy"—2 Timothy 1:3-4. Paul and Timothy were very close friends—almost like father and son. In his two letters to Timothy, Paul told him over and over how much he meant to him and encouraged him to do the right thing and "fight the good fight, holding on to faith and a good conscience" (1 Timothy 1:18-19). When they were apart, Paul longed for the joy of being with Timothy again. Great friends—best friends forever—are like that.

CPSIA information can be obtained at www.ICGtesting.com

261865BV00001B/6/P